COLLECTION EDITOR: **JENNIFER GRÜNWALD**
ASSISTANT EDITOR: **SARAH BRUNSTAD**
ASSOCIATE MANAGING EDITOR: **ALEX STARBUCK**
EDITOR, SPECIAL PROJECTS: **MARK D. BEAZLEY**
SENIOR EDITOR, SPECIAL PROJECTS: **JEFF YOUNGQUIST**
SVP PRINT, SALES & MARKETING: **DAVID GABRIEL**
BOOK DESIGN: **JEFF POWELL**

EDITOR IN CHIEF: **AXEL ALONSO**
CHIEF CREATIVE OFFICER: **JOE QUESADA**
PUBLISHER: **DAN BUCKLEY**
EXECUTIVE PRODUCER: **ALAN FINE**

NEW AVENGERS VOL. 4: A PERFECT WORLD. Contains material originally published in magazine form as NEW AVENGERS #18-23. First printing 2014. ISBN# 978-0-7851-5485-3. Published by MARVEL WORLDWIDE, INC., a subsidiary of MARVEL ENTERTAINMENT, LLC. OFFICE OF PUBLICATION: 135 West 50th Street, New York, NY 10020. Copyright © 2014 Marvel Characters, Inc. All rights reserved. All characters featured in this issue and the distinctive names and likenesses thereof, and all related indicia are trademarks of Marvel Characters, Inc. No similarity between any of the names, characters, persons, and/or institutions in this magazine with those of any living or dead person or institution is intended, and any such similarity which may exist is purely coincidental. **Printed in the U.S.A.** ALAN FINE, EVP - Office of the President, Marvel Worldwide, Inc. and EVP & CMO Marvel Characters B.V.; DAN BUCKLEY, Publisher & President - Print, Animation & Digital Divisions; JOE QUESADA, Chief Creative Officer; TOM BREVOORT, SVP of Publishing; DAVID BOGART, SVP of Operations & Procurement, Publishing; C.B. CEBULSKI, SVP of Creator & Content Development; DAVID GABRIEL, SVP Print, Sales & Marketing; JIM O'KEEFE, VP of Operations & Logistics; DAN CARR, Executive Director of Publishing Technology; SUSAN CRESPI, Editorial Operations Manager; ALEX MORALES, Publishing Operations Manager; STAN LEE, Chairman Emeritus. For information regarding advertising in Marvel Comics or on Marvel.com, please contact Niza Disla, Director of Marvel Partnerships, at ndisla@marvel.com. For Marvel subscription inquiries, please call 800-217-9158. **Manufactured between 9/5/2014 and 10/20/2014 by R.R. DONNELLEY, INC., SALEM, VA, USA.**

WRITER: **JONATHAN HICKMAN**

ISSUES #18-21

ARTIST: **VALERIO SCHITI** WITH SALVADOR LARROCA (#21)

COLOR ARTIST: **FRANK MARTIN** WITH PAUL MOUNTS (#20-21)

COVER ART: **DUSTIN WEAVER & JASON KEITH**

ISSUES #22-23

ARTIST: **KEV WALKER**

COLOR ARTIST: **FRANK MARTIN**

COVER ART: **DALE KEOWN & JASON KEITH** (#22) AND
CHRISTIAN WARD (#23)

AS A RESULT OF THE TERRIGEN BOMB, YOUR POWERS ARE GREATLY REDUCED. I WOULDN'T SAY BLACK BOLT IS HALF THE MAN HE WAS, BUT...

...WE'LL HAVE TO HIDE THIS.

T'CHALLA, WAKANDA CANNOT WIN A WAR WITH ATLANTIS.

NAMOR, YOU'RE WRONG.

AND MEN CALL *ME* ARROGANT. TELL YOUR SISTER, THE QUEEN, I WILL OFFER FAVORABLE TERMS. I ASK ONLY FOR THE CESSATION OF HOSTILITIES.

SHE WILL REFUSE.

THEN SHE IS A FOOL.

SO YOU ARE SELLING YOUR SOUL, STEPHEN?

IF I AM TO BE DAMNED, LET IT BE USING ALL THE RESOURCES AT THE DISPOSAL OF A SORCERER SUPREME.

HOW MUCH OF YOUR SOUL DO YOU SELL THIS DAY?

ALL OF IT.

YOU SHOULDN'T FEEL GUILTY, BRUCE. YOUR SOCIOPATHIC OTHER-DIMENSIONAL COUNTERPART WAS A KILLER...

WE'RE PLAYING FOR EVERYTHING. WELCOME TO THE CLUB.

ON AN ALTERNATE EARTH AN EVENT OCCURRED THAT CAUSED THE EARLY DEATH OF A UNIVERSE. THIS CAUSED A TINY CONTRACTION, SMASHING TWO UNIVERSES TOGETHER AT THE INCURSION POINT OF THE INITIAL EVENT, EARTH.

AFTER AN INCURSION, EITHER BOTH EARTHS ARE DESTROYED OR ONE IS SACRIFICED, SPARING BOTH UNIVERSES.

BLACK SWAN, YOU CAME FROM ANOTHER WORLD WITH A DEVICE, THEN DESTROYED THAT PLANET.

WHAT YOU *NEED* IS A *MIRROR* TO OBSERVE ANY NUMBER OF INEVITABLE ADVERSARIES.

WHAT YOU CALL A MIRROR, I CALL A BRIDGE. I CAN BUILD IT. I'VE ACTUALLY BUILT ONE BEFORE.

YOU UNDERSTAND. IF YOU USE THE MIRROR AND FOCUS YOUR NEEDS YOU CAN OBSERVE OTHER INCURSIONS AS THEY ARE OCCURRING.

"ARE WE LOOKING AT A PAST EVENT?"

"NO. WE'RE LOOKING AT THE FUTURE. *TWO HOURS FROM NOW*."

THE ILLUMINATI

BLACK BOLT
Celestial Messiah

NAMOR
Imperius Rex

REED RICHARDS
Universal Builder

IRON MAN
Master of Machines

BEAST
Mutant Genius

DOCTOR STRANGE
Sorcerer Supreme

BLACK PANTHER
King of the Dead

HULK/BRUCE BANNER
Strongest There Is

BLACK SWAN
Incursion Survivor

MAXIMUS
Inhuman Madman

BOUNDLESS

DR. SPECTRUM

SUN GOD

THE RIDER

THE JOVIAN

THE NORN

"INTO THE BREACH"

WOOF!

YES... YOU'RE RIGHT, LOCKJAW. INDEED YOU ARE.

HE *IS* GETTING STRONGER...

BLACK BOLT IS HEALING.

RIGHT NOW, EVEN AS WE WATCH, SCARRED AND DAMAGED TISSUE IS BEING REGENERATED IN THOSE EXOGENETICALLY CHARGED WATERS.

WOOF!

YES, OF COURSE IT HURTS-- RAPID HEALING ALWAYS HAS A COST...NOT THAT OUR KING HASN'T ALWAYS BEEN SOMETHING OF A MASOCHIST.

MY BROTHER, YOU SEE--THE CELESTIAL MESSIAH--HUNG HIMSELF ON THE CROSS SO THAT OUR PEOPLE MIGHT BE SAVED THROUGH GLOBAL TERRIGENESIS.

AND NOW WE'RE ALL ONE HAPPY UNIVERSAL FAMILY OF INHUMANS.

WELL, WE ARE IF YOU OVERLOOK THE FACT THAT, RIGHT NOW, EVERYONE THINKS WE DIED IN THE FALL OF ATTILAN.

STILL, WE HAVE OUR PLANS... AND NOW WE HAVE A FIT AND FULLY HEALED KING.

ALL HE HAS TO DO IS RETURN VICTORIOUS FROM THE ILLUMINATI'S WAR TO ANSWER THE NIGHTLY PRAYERS OF HIS PEOPLE.

THEY WILL ACCEPT OUR RESURRECTION WITH OPEN ARMS...

FOR WHAT SANE PERSON WANTS TO COMMUNE WITH THE DEAD?

IT'S NOT WEAKNESS.

IT'S NOT.

NOR IS IT DOUBT.

I KNOW WHO I AM.

BUT THE VERY IDEA OF KNOWLEDGE IS THAT IF YOU HAVE ENOUGH INFORMATION-- IF YOU HAVE ACCUMULATED ENOUGH DATA TO ACCURATELY MAKE A DECISION--THEN YOU CAN SOMEHOW...MANAGE YOUR FATE.

AND MANAGE THE FATE OF YOUR PEOPLE.

SO I THOUGHT KNOWING WHAT WE WERE UP AGAINST WOULD, IN SOME MANNER, MAKE THINGS EASIER...

MOVE ALL THIS-- WHAT WE MUST DO-- PAST THE HOPE AND LUCK ON WHICH WE HAVE SUSTAINED OURSELVES TO SOMETHING FIRMER.

BUT I HAVE SEEN WHAT IS COMING NEXT...

I FEAR FOR MY SOUL...AND THE FUTURE OF OUR PEOPLE.

YOU CAN SPEAK PLAINLY, T'CHALLA...

THERE IS NO NEED FOR SUCH FORMALITY... OR SUBTLETY.

AFTER ALL, ARE WE NOT NOW ALL ONE?

BUT LOOK IN THOSE EYES, THE BOY KING HAS SEEN SOMETHING THAT'S SHAMED HIM...

HAVE YOU BEEN WEEPING, PRINCE?

PFFAH! WE DEAD SHOULD BE BEYOND RIDICULING THE LIVING.

AND YET HERE I AM...AS I AM, HUNTING BONES LIKE THE REST OF YOU.

TELL US, T'CHALLA... WHAT ARE YOU AFRAID OF?

"THEN YOU KNOW--THE GREAT GOLDEN CITY, GREATER THAN ANY OTHER IN THE WORLD...

"HOW MANY COULD WE HAVE HELPED--HOW MANY COULD WE HAVE SAVED--IF WE CHOSE NOT TO BE HIDDEN... NOT TO BE SET APART?"

"MANY TIMES BECAUSE WE DID NOTHING, MEN, WOMEN AND CHILDREN DIED...

"AND WE DID THIS BECAUSE IT WAS BEST FOR OUR PEOPLE AND WAKANDA."

THAT IS A KING'S MORALITY.

WE HAVE ALL MADE IMPOSSIBLE CHOICES LIKE THE ONES FACING YOU.

BUT WE SHOULDER THEM AS WE SHOULD... IT IS OUR BURDEN.

YOU SOUGHT OUR COUNSEL AND HERE IT IS: MEASURE ALL THINGS AGAINST THE SURVIVAL OF OUR PEOPLE. AND THAT SURVIVAL ABOVE ALL OTHERS.

WILL THERE BE A COST? YES. MIGHT THE UNIVERSE BURN? LET IT.

THESE ARE HARD WORDS TO HEAR, BUT YOU MUST HEAR THEM ALL THE SAME.

YOU WILL KILL THEM ALL IF IT MEANS WAKANDA STANDS.

THE GOLDEN CITY MUST NEVER FALL.

I WILL DO...

...WHAT I MUST.

WELCOME BACK, STEPHEN... YOU'RE JUST IN TIME.

FFFT

WELL...DON'T *YOU* LOOK LIKE A MAN WHO'S JUST HAD AN EXPERIENCE?

OH...I GET IT.

ANTIMATTER INJECTOR BUILT TO PIERCE THE CORE AND CAUSE A VIRTUALLY INSTANTANEOUS PLANETARY EXPLOSION.

IT REALLY IS SOME FEAT OF ENGINEERING.

MY QUESTION IS...WHY SO MANY?

AND WHY DO YOU SEEM TO BE ARMING ONE?

I CAN GUESS, OF COURSE...BUT I DON'T THINK I'LL LIKE THE ANSWER.

NO ONE DOES, DOCTOR BANNER.

AND FORGIVE MY OUT-OF-CHARACTER BLUNTNESS AS I EXPAND ON THE THEME...

BUT I KNOW ANTHONY DIDN'T BRING YOU IN WITHOUT EXPLAINING THAT THE PROBLEM ISN'T A SINGLE END-TIMES SCENARIO REQUIRING A ONE-TIME SUPER-GENIUS SOLUTION.

IT'S A VARIATION OF THAT IMPOSSIBLE PROBLEM AN INFINITE NUMBER OF TIMES.

... HERE'S WHAT'S GOING TO HAPPEN NEXT:

WE'RE GOING TO DEAL WITH THIS UPCOMING INCURSION.

THEN I'M GOING TO TALK TO THE OTHERS--DO WHATEVER IT TAKES TO CONVINCE THEM WE NEED TO BRING IN SOMEONE WHO CAN DIG AROUND IN YOUR MIND.

BYPASS ALL THE GAMES, ALL THE LIES, AND GET RIGHT TO THE TRUTH.

THE TRUTH? I'VE NEVER LIED TO ANY OF YOU.

EVER HEARD OF LIES OF OMISSION, SWAN?

YES. THAT'S WHAT ALL THE IGNORANT PEOPLE CALL DISPLAYS OF THEIR IGNORANCE.

TONY. IT'S TIME. INCURSION'S TWENTY MINUTES OUT.

WE HAVE TO GO.

AND YOU'RE SURE OF WHAT YOU SAW?

YOU'VE WATCHED THE RECORDINGS FROM THE BRIDGE AS WELL...

WE'RE ALL SURE OF WHAT'S WAITING FOR US ON THAT OTHER WORLD...

"WE HAVE SEEN SO MUCH EVIL IN THE COLLAPSING OF WORLDS...BUT NOW WE WILL SEE SOMETHING TRULY WICKED.

"WHAT'S WORSE THAN FACING VILLAINS WITH THE FATE OF YOUR WORLD HANGING IN THE BALANCE?

"WE ARE ALL MONSTERS NOW"

INCURSION.
EARTH-616 : EARTH-4,290,001.

ANYTHING?

THEN.

WHAT'S THIS, DOCTOR BANNER?

AN IDEA I GOT FROM THE BRAIN-DAMAGED HULK FROM ANOTHER EARTH...

HIS AVENGERS TEAMMATES COULD CONTROL HIM BY STIMULATING THE EMOTIONAL CENTERS OF HIS BRAIN. THEY BASICALLY CREATED A HULK OVERRIDE SYSTEM--CONTROLLING WHEN HE COULD BECOME THE HULK AND WHEN HE REMAINED BANNER.

A SLIGHT PINCH.

PFPTT!

OW.

ANYWAY... THIS IS MY VERSION OF THAT.

IT'S A LIMITED WORK-AROUND THAT I'LL USE SPARINGLY...

BUT IT GIVES ME SOME MANNER OF CONTROL OVER WHEN I CHANGE--AND, FOR LACK OF A BETTER TERM, IT ALLOWS ME TO THROTTLE BACK WHILE GREEN WITH RAGE.

WELL, PARDON ME FOR STATING THE OBVIOUS, BRUCE... BUT WHY THE LIMITATION?

IF IT WORKS, IT WORKS... NO?

WELL...IT WORKS BY FIRING ELECTRICITY INTO SOME RATHER DELICATE AREAS OF MY BRAIN, DR. McCOY. SO...

YOU'D RATHER NOT LOBOTOMIZE YOURSELF.

ESPECIALLY SINCE WE'RE HERE FIRST AND FOREMOST FOR THAT VERY THING.

IF YOU SAY SO...

I'M BEGINNING TO WONDER HOW TRUE THAT REALLY IS.

I'M NEW HERE, HANK.

NEBULOUS HINTS AT SECRET MOTIVATIONS JUST LEAVE ME WONDERING WHAT YOU'RE TALKING ABOUT.

WITH THE TWO OF US, THERE'S STILL ENOUGH BRAIN ACTIVITY IN OUR SECRET ORGANIZATION TO POWER A SMALL CITY.

ALL THESE QUESTIONS WE BRILLIANT MEN ARE ASKING...

WHAT IF THEY'RE NOT THE RIGHT QUESTIONS AT ALL?

GO ON...I'M LISTENING.

WHAT IF--IN THE END-- THIS ISN'T AN EXERCISE IN SURVIVAL, BRUCE, BUT A QUESTION OF HUMANITY?

YOU TELL ME...

WHO HERE KNOWS BETTER THAN YOU AND I...THE REALITY OF THAT STRUGGLE...

AND HOW EASILY THE HUMAN GIVES WAY TO SOMETHING LESS MORAL AND MORE PRIMAL.

LIVING IN A VIOLENT WORLD MAKES ONE QUESTION THE GOODNESS OF MAN. YET YOU CAME HERE, WITH YOUR ARMS WIDE OPEN...

TALKING *PEACE* WHILE THE SKY BLEEDS RED.

SEE? THERE *IS* HOPE.

STILL...

A PEACEFUL ARRIVAL UNDER A WHITE FLAG AND PASSING SOME MAGICAL RORSCHACH TEST ISN'T REALLY A GUARANTEE OF ANYTHING, IS IT?

HOW *CAN* WE REALLY TRUST YOU?

MORE IMPORTANTLY... HOW DO *YOU* KNOW TO TRUST *US*?

OH, WE'VE BEEN WATCHING YOU.

WHAT?

WE'VE BEEN *WATCHING* YOU.

SAYING IT AGAIN DOESN'T MAKE IT BETTER.

CREEP.

NO, YOU DON'T UNDERSTAND... WE CONSTRUCTED A MACHINE THAT ENABLED US TO OBSERVE YOUR EARTH.

WE USED THIS MACHINE TO STUDY MULTIPLE EARTHS UNDERGOING INCURSIONS... SO WE USED IT TO STUDY YOU.

I THINK THEY GET IT, HENRY.

YOU HAVE SEEN THE END OF WORLDS?

TOO MANY TIMES.

AND YOU?

THREE.

THREE TIMES.

INTERESTING. WE WERE ONLY ABLE TO OBSERVE AND RECORD *TWO*.

YES. WHILE YOUR MAPMAKER SOLUTION WAS LESS THAN ELEGANT, THE OTHER INSTANCE WE OBSERVED WAS FASCINATING...

IN FACT, ALL OUR MODELS SEEMED TO IMPLY THAT WHAT YOU DID *WASN'T POSSIBLE*.

HOW DID YOU MOVE YOUR EARTH-- AND BY EXTENSION YOUR UNIVERSE-- OUT OF PHASE?

I USED A *WISHING BOX*.

WHAT IS--

WHOOMP!

IT'S AN ITEM OF GREAT POWER, A CUBE MADE UP OF SIX PLANES OF FOREVER GLASS.

BUT THAT IS LOST TO US NOW, AS THE BOX WAS DESTROYED IN THE PROCESS.

OH. I SEE.

YOU UNDERSTAND? YOU HAVE SEEN A *WISHING BOX* BEFORE?

A DIFFERENT MANIFESTATION OF IT. WE CALLED OURS A *GAUNTLET*. IT HAD INFINITY GEMS, NOT PLANES OF... FOREVER GLASS.

I SUPPOSE THERE'S SOME COMFORT IN KNOWING THAT WAS NEVER A LONG-TERM SOLUTION.

WHAT WAS THE THIRD?

WE DON'T TALK ABOUT THAT.

SO, THEORETICS ASIDE...WHAT ARE YOU GOING TO DO ABOUT THIS INCURSION?

WHAT PLANS DO YOU HAVE?

WE HAVE NO PLANS--WHAT PLANS COULD ANYONE HAVE FOR SOMETHING LIKE THIS?

DO YOU HAVE PLANS?

YOU KNOW WHAT...WHY DON'T WE TALK ABOUT OPTIONS INSTEAD OF WORSE-CASE SCENARIOS?

SEE IF WE CAN'T COME UP WITH SOMETHING IN THE TIME WE HAVE LEFT.

YOU DO HAVE A PLAN. YOU JUST DON'T WANT TO TELL US.

YOU'RE HIDING SOMETHING...

YES. WE HAVE A PLAN.

IT'S AN ANTIMATTER DEVICE THAT WILL DESTROY A PLANET. WE HAVE A *BOMB*.

WE BUILT A BOMB THAT WILL DESTROY A WORLD.

ARE YOU SURE YOU DON'T HAVE ANYTHING ELSE?

I TOLD YOU ALREADY... WE HAVE *HOPE*.

WELL... I *HOPE* YOU CAN COME UP WITH SOMETHING BETTER.

"EVERYONE AROUND HERE IS CONCERNED ABOUT RUNNING OUT OF TIME.

"I SAY THE TICKING CLOCK MAKES US LESS WASTEFUL. I SAY THE CLOCK MAKES US BOLD."

I SAY IT'S TIME TO GET A LITTLE CRAZY.

WHAT ABOUT YOU, LITTLE BIRD?

I THINK, FOR A MAN OF ACTION, YOU TALK TOO MUCH, MAXIMUS.

YES, YOU'RE RIGHT, OF COURSE. SO... FORWARD WITH THE EXPERIMENT.

THEY NEVER LET ME PLAY WITH THE GOOD TOYS...SO I HAVE TO WAIT UNTIL ALL THE COWBOYS ARE AWAY AT THE ROW-DEE-OH.

MICROSCOPIC DRILL-- WE DON'T WANT ANY PRYING EYES TO SEE THE HOLE...

BUT I'M DYING TO KNOW WHAT HAPPENS WHEN A LITTLE AIR REACHES THOSE REGROWING BONES OF *CORVUS GLAIVE.*

OH MY... HE DIDN'T DISAPPOINT, DID HE?

THEN.

WANT TO TELL ME WHAT THAT WAS ABOUT?

A MAN COMING TO THE END OF HIMSELF.

YOU *DO* KNOW THAT THERE'S NOTHING ABNORMAL ABOUT HOW HUMAN BEINGS RESPOND TO TRAUMA, DON'T YOU, SWAN?

THIS JUDGING PEOPLE FOR THEIR WEAKNESSES IN THE FACE OF TRAGEDY-- IT'S COUNTER TO EVERYTHING WE KNOW ABOUT HOW PEOPLE DEAL WITH PAIN.

ARE YOU SAYING THAT ANTHONY IS IN PAIN?

WE ALL ARE, INCLUDING YOU. YOU'VE JUST BEEN HURTING A LOT LONGER...AND IT'S MADE YOU MUCH, MUCH HARDER.

I'VE SAID IT BEFORE, AND I'LL SAY IT AGAIN...I CAN HELP YOU.

AND?

YOU KNOW I HAVE KNOWN OTHER YOUS...AND I HAVE HEARD THEM SAY SIMILAR THINGS...

I'VE LEARNED THIS IS HOW THE GREAT REED RICHARDS MANAGES *HIS PAIN.*

APPEALING TO THE HEART WHEN HIS INTELLECT HAS FAILED.

THIS.

THIS IS WHEN YOU NO LONGER INTEREST ME, REED...

BECAUSE YOU BECOME USELESS.

YES.
WHAT *ABOUT* THE OTHERS?

THERE'S NO GOING BACK NOW.

AND GOING FORWARD...MY GOD, THE FULL WEIGHT OF THE *MOST POWERFUL AVENGERS TEAM EVER ASSEMBLED* IS GETTING READY TO COME CRASHING DOWN ON US.

SO THAT'S WHY, IN THERE, YOU WERE THREATENING TO DO WHAT YOU--

YEAH.
I DON'T KNOW WHAT TO DO ANY MORE... DO YOU?

BEYOND OUR CONTINGENCIES--THE NIGHTMARE SCENARIOS THAT WE'RE MOVING TOWARDS? NO.

THE WORST PART IS THEY'LL BE RIGHTEOUS IN COMING AFTER US. WE'VE DONE TERRIBLE THINGS, ANTHONY.

AND THE WORST OF IT ALL...

WE *CAN'T STOP*, CAN WE?

NOW.

SO WHAT WAS YOUR PLAN?

COME HERE? KILL US? BLOW UP OUR WORLD?

SOME OTHER SEDUCTIVE DANCE MEANT TO CATCH US UNAWARES?

WAYNE, I'M SURE THAT--

NO. WE NEED TO KNOW THIS. NOW.

ARE YOU HERE TO KILL OUR WORLD?

OF COURSE NOT.

OF COURSE NOT.

BECAUSE WE WANT TO BELIEVE WE'RE NOT ALL CAPABLE OF THE UNTHINKABLE.

NAMOR--DON'T SAY ANOTHER WORD.

LISTEN. WE HAVE TIME.

NOT MUCH, BUT SOME...WHAT WE NEED TO FOCUS ON IS FIGURING OUT A WAY TO SAVE THE MOST PEOPLE.

YOU MAKE IT SOUND LIKE TRIAGE.

IT IS!

HONESTLY, WHAT ELSE *COULD* IT BE?

TWO UNIVERSES COLLIDING AT THE TOUCH POINT OF EARTHS-- THE ONLY WAY TO SAVE THEM IS FOR ONE OF THOSE EARTHS TO BE DESTROYED...SAVING BOTH UNIVERSES.

AND A SINGLE EARTH.

ALL THAT REMAINS IS CHOOSING WHICH ONE. IT WOULD BE WRONG--IT WOULD BE *IMMORAL*-- NOT TO MAKE A CHOICE.

IF YOU'RE ATTEMPTING TO CONSTRUCT AN ARGUMENT THAT MAKES YOU THE MOST MORAL MASS-MURDERER IN THE LONG HISTORY OF MASS-MURDERERS...CONGRATULATIONS. YOU'VE SUCCEEDED.

ARE YOU PROUD OF YOURSELF?

NORN...AN ASSESSMENT, PLEASE.

THERE ARE NO LIES HERE. ONLY REGRET.

THERE IS A SHADE OVER THESE MEN'S SOULS...BUT THAT HAS NOT ALWAYS BEEN THE CASE. HOWEVER, NOW THEY GRAVITATE TO THE NIGHT.

GREAT BUILDERS OF WEAPONS. MACHINES OF DESTRUCTION. WORDS OF POWER. SOUNDS OF FURY.

A STORM TO CONSUME US ALL...

SO YOU'RE PROPOSING WHAT, EXACTLY?

THAT WE WORK TOGETHER TO FIND SOME SOLUTION OVER THE NEXT HOUR, AND IF WE DO NOT FIND ONE, WE MOVE ON TO WORST-CASE SCENARIOS.

LET'S DO THAT.

NO. I WANT TO TALK ABOUT YOUR... WORST-CASE SCENARIOS.

LET'S ASSUME WE FAIL. TELL ME WHAT'S GOING TO HAPPEN.

SOMETHING TERRIBLE.

BE MORE SPECIFIC.

IN ORDER TO SAVE BOTH UNIVERSES... AN EARTH HAS TO DIE. YOU KNOW THIS.

I DO... BUT WHICH EARTH?

I DON'T KNOW.

I THINK YOU DO...BUT EVEN IF YOU DON'T...

GIVE ME YOUR BEST GUESS.

DO YOU HAVE THE POWER TO DESTROY A PLANET?

NO. BUT YOU DO.

YES. WE DO.

BUT WE SHOULD BE--

NO! BECAUSE IF YOU THINK ABOUT IT...THERE'S ONLY ONE OF TWO OPTIONS; YOU KILL OUR EARTH...OR YOU KILL YOUR OWN.

SO YOU LISTEN TO ME! YOU'RE NOT KILLING OUR WORLD, NOT WHILE I STILL BREATHE...

NOT WHILE ANY OF US DO!

THUNK!

I'M TIRED OF WAITING FOR THE INEVITABLE. IF I MUST BECOME THIS THING, THEN LET IT BE AT A TIME OF MY OWN CHOOSING.

WAYNE! WAYNE! ARE YOU...

STILL BREATHING. BUT YOU UNDERSTAND NOW, RIGHT? THIS CAN'T END ANY OTHER WAY.

YES.

OH, GOD...

THIS IS IT.

"BLU'DAKORR"

WHY? WHY DID YOU STOP?

I HELD IT IN MY HANDS...THE POWER TO CREATE AND DESTROY WORLDS...

WHY?

WE HAD A DEAL.

DEALS ARE SEALED WITH TRUST. A SURETY THAT WITHSTANDS THE TRANSACTION.

WHAT DO YOU CALL A DEAL WHERE ONE SIDE CANNOT MEET THE OBLIGATIONS?

NO DEAL AT ALL.

STEPHEN STRANGE...YOU ARE A DEBTOR. INSOLVENT.

A BANKRUPT LIAR.

HOW COULD YOU OFFER YOUR SOUL AS PAYMENT, SORCERER...

WHEN YOU LACK THE FULL MEASURE OF ONE?

NOW.

WE'RE COMMITTED NOW...HERE THEY COME!

STEPHEN! WHAT'S THE STATUS OF HANK AND REED?

THEY'RE OUT...

BUT I SEE NO INTERNAL BLEEDING. AND NO BROKEN BONES OR HEAD TRAUMA.

THEY'LL BE FINE AS LONG AS--

AARGGGHHHH!

THIS ONE... HAS POWER BUT DOES NOT GUARD HIS MIND. WITHIN I SEE A POISONED HEART. I SEE TWISTED THOUGHTS.

I SEE PLANS, DARK PLANS.

I SEE THEIR WEAPON.

WE ALREADY KNOW ABOUT THE BOMB, NORN...

IT DOESN'T DO US ANY GOOD IF WE DON'T KNOW THE DAMN THING'S LOCATION.

FIND IT!

FARCASTING THE SPHERE YIELDS NO RESONANCE.

HOW DO YOU HIDE SOMETHING THAT IS SOMETHING AND NOT NOTHING?

UNLESS... YES...

THE SECOND SPHERE.

"THEY LEFT THE BOMB ON THEIR WORLD--AT THEIR INCURSION POINT."

FOR QUICK RETRIEVAL, NO DOUBT.

SPECTRUM! GO! NOW!

"YOU HAVE TO DESTROY THE BOMB!"

I'M ON IT... BUT I'M NOT THE ONLY ONE, I SEE.

HURK!

YES. THE PAIN IS UNFORTUNATE... BUT THAT'S WHAT IT'S COME TO, HASN'T IT?

YOU FIGHT AND CLAW AND BITE FOR ANOTHER BREATH, BUT IT WON'T DO YOU ANY GOOD. NOT AGAINST ME.

I'VE WATCHED YOU...HOW YOU FIGHT...HOW YOU THINK...

WHILE YOU HAVE NO IDEA WHAT YOU'RE FACING.

YOU'RE WRONG. I MAY NOT KNOW YOU...I MAY HAVE NEVER SEEN YOU BEFORE...

BUT I'VE SEEN YOUR KIND: FLAWED MEN FEIGNING NOBILITY.

ANY PAIN I FEEL IS OUT OF PITY...

I FEEL SORRY FOR YOU.

AND THE WRETCHED END YOU MUST HAVE WAITING FOR YOU.

LOOK AT YOU...POWERFUL... RECKLESS AND DANGEROUS.

THE PERFECT EMBODIMENT OF WHAT SEEMS TO BE THE TRAIT YOU "HEROES" SHARE.

YOU'RE ALL *OUT OF CONTROL*...LIKE SOME CORRUPTED FORCE OF NATURE.

HULK NOT OUT OF CONTROL!

HULK NOT NATURE!

HULK IS THE STRONGEST ONE THERE IS!

BLACK PANTHER: ENGAGED (STALEMATE)
NAMOR: ENGAGED (STALEMATE)
MISTER FANTASTIC: INACTIVE (UNCONSCIOUS)
BEAST: INACTIVE (UNCONSCIOUS)
HULK: INACTIVE (DEFEATED)
BLACK BOLT: DISENGAGED (OFFWORLD)
DOCTOR STRANGE: ENGAGED (UNKNOWN)

OH, GOD...

IRON MAN STATUS: ENGAGED
TARGET: BOUNDLESS.
(TRACKING SYSTEM / TARGETING OFFLINE)
(SYSTEM FAILURE IMMINENT)

DO YOU NEED ANY HELP, BOUNDLESS?

YOU DO NOT NEED AN ALL-SEEING EYE TO UNDERSTAND WHAT HAS HAPPENED HERE TODAY, SORCERER...

VIRTUE CANNOT BE BARTERED. YES, WE MAY DO EVIL THINGS FOR A GREATER GOOD...

THAT IS AN ACCEPTABLE PRICE...

BUT THE *UNTHINKABLE?*

THE VERY *IDEA* IS UNSPEAKABLE AND MUST NOT BE UTTERED.

SO I SAY NOW TO YOU...*OTHER THINGS.*

DO YOU KNOW THE WORDS OF THE *BLACK PRIESTS,* SORCERER SUPREME?

HAVE YOU HEARD THEM?

K'OOTH UL D'AYN.

YOOL D'AYN HAT WHUURL.

THEN.

I AM DAMNED...AND WORSE THAN THAT, SOMEWHERE ALONG THE WAY I HAVE BECOME *LOST.*

TELL ME, WONG...IF I AM LOST, AND LACKING BOTH TIME AND MEANS... THEN WHAT HOPE DO I HAVE FOR REDEMPTION?

WE DO WORKS FOR MANY REASONS, MASTER.

I THINK, FOR A SEASON, YOU HAVE CHOSEN TO WALK THIS WORLD AND OTHERS WITH YOUR EYES CLOSED...

AND NOW YOU ASK ME--HOW CAN I CONTINUE IF I HAVE BECOME BLIND?

OPEN YOUR EYES, MY FRIEND. SEE THE THINGS THAT I KNOW ARE REAL...AND BELIEVE TO BE TRUE.

AND WHAT ARE THOSE?

YOU, STEPHEN.

SOMEWHERE IN THERE...YOU ARE STILL A GOOD MAN.

THEN LET THAT SLIVER OF WHAT I WAS BE ENOUGH...

AS ALL I SEE BEFORE ME NOW IS *THE ABYSS.*

AND WHAT LIVES THERE... WHICH WILL LIVE THROUGH ME.

K'OOTH UL D'AYN. YOOL--

--D'AYN HAT WHUURL.

DO YOU KNOW THESE WORDS, CHARLATAN?

OF COURSE YOU DON'T.

YOU DON'T EVEN HAVE *THE GIFT*, DO YOU?

I WOULD WAGER YOU'VE SPENT MOST OF YOUR LIFE ACQUIRING YOUR ITEMS OF POWER. AT BEST, YOU'RE A CURATOR...

NO!

BUT I THINK WE BOTH KNOW YOU'RE JUST A THIEF.

UNF!

WOULD YOU LIKE TO SEE *REAL* POWER, CHILD?

WOULD YOU LIKE TO SEE WHAT THE *ART* REALLY COSTS?

K'OOTH
UL D'AYN...

"YOOL D'AYN HAT WHUURL."

AAIIEEE!

AARGHH! ZORAN! LOOK OUT!

WHAT IS THIS?

WHAT HAVE YOU DONE, SORCERER? WHAT HAVE YOU DONE?

"THE BOMB"

THEN.
THE NECROPOLIS.
WAKANDA.

T'CHALLA...

YES, FATHER?

WHY DOES THE ATLANTEAN STILL BREATHE?

WHY HAVEN'T YOU KILLED HIM YET?

WHY HAVEN'T YOU DONE WHAT YOU PROMISED?

WHAT I PROMISED? I HAVE DONE EVERYTHING THAT COULD BE EXPECTED OF ME--SACRIFICED EVERYTHING FOR MY PEOPLE... EVERYTHING FOR MY NATION.

MY OWN DESIRES, MY OWN MARRIAGE...I HAVE COMMITTED MURDER MANY, MANY TIMES.

"YOOL D'AYN HAT WHUURL.

"YOOL D'AYN HAT WHUURL!"

WAYNE!

ACK!

YOU...YOU WERE RIGHT, ZORAN. I WAS WRONG.

IF IT ALL ENDS THIS BADLY, I SHOULD HAVE LIVED A BETT--

AARGGHH!

NO... WAYNE... NO...

I HAVE DONE ALL OF THIS FOR WAKANDA--WITH HEAD HELD HIGH, AND NO REGARD FOR SELF...

HOW *DARE* YOU DOUBT ME, FATHER.

MY SON... HERE IN THE SHADOWLANDS--BEYOND ALL MORTAL CONCERNS AND CONSTRAINTS--I SEE ONLY TWO THINGS: WHAT IS DONE. WHAT IS NOT DONE.

SO AM I BLIND? IS THE ATLANTEAN A WELL-PRESERVED CORPSE YOU USE AS A MARIONETTE? OR DOES HE YET LIVE...ARROGANT AND UNPUNISHED?

BLOOD DEMANDS BLOOD, T'CHALLA--DO YOUR DUTY.

I AM TRYING TO SAVE *OUR PEOPLE*, FATHER--*THAT IS MY DUTY!*

AND WHILE I STILL LIVE, I WILL NOT LOOK AT THE WORLD AND SEE ALL PEOPLE AS YOU DO--EVENTUAL ASH AND DUST--BUT AS MEN AND WOMEN WHO STILL BREATHE, AND HAVE PURPOSE.

I BELIEVE NAMOR HAS A PURPOSE.

AND UNTIL THAT PURPOSE HAS BEEN FULFILLED... HE WILL HAVE MY MERCY.

MERCY? *MERCY?*

MY FOOLISH SON. FOR A KING... EVERY MOMENT OF MERCY IS A *TRAGEDY.*

K'OOTH
UL D'AYN.

"YOOL
D'AYN HAT
WHUURL."

AARRGGHHH!

NOOO!

HURK!

ARRGGHH—

HHHHHHH

HHHHH

DO WE HAVE ANY IDEA IF WHAT HE IS DOING IS GOING TO SAVE EARTH...

OR ANYTHING AT ALL?

I DON'T KNOW HOW WE COULD. THAT MONSTER IS...

NO.

WAKANDA.
THE NECROPOLIS.

"I THINK I'VE FIGURED IT OUT..."

"DO YOU KNOW WHAT YOUR PROBLEM IS?"

WHY DON'T YOU TELL ME?

I SAY PROBLEM LIKE IT'S ONE THING-- SINGULAR--BUT IT'S ACTUALLY A COMBINATION OF THINGS. WHICH I PROBABLY SHOULDN'T BOTHER POINTING OUT, AS MOST PROBLEMS ARE ACTUALLY "MULTIPLE PROBLEMS"...

A SERIES OF COMPLICATIONS THAT EVENTUALLY REACH A CRITICAL, NONDISSIPATING STATE THAT INEVITABLY LEADS TO--

IT REALLY IS STUNNING HOW MUCH YOU LOVE TO HEAR YOURSELF TALK, MAXIMUS.

YOU WANT ME TO GET TO THE POINT. I CAN DO THAT.

"YOUR PROBLEM IS ONE OF *EXCLUSION*, AND IT'S ALSO ONE OF *EXPERIENCE*...

"SEE, I WENT BACK AND LOOKED AT THE LOGS OF YOUR--AND OTHER SWANS'--ADVENTURES THROUGH SPACE AND TIME, AND SOMETHING JUMPED OUT AT ME...YOU BIRDS HAVE A PATTERN.

"YOU RECRUIT A CERTAIN TYPE OF PERSON TO HELP YOU DO WHATEVER IT IS THAT YOU'RE SUPPOSED TO DO.

"YOU RECRUIT *HEROES*.

"PROBABLY SOMETHING TO DO WITH EXPLOITABLE IDEALISM AND THE FREQUENTLY TERMINAL AFFLICTION CALLED ALTRUISM.

"BUT THAT'S NOT WHAT YOU DID HERE ON *OUR* EARTH...SEE, THAT'S WHAT YOU WANTED...BUT YOU GOT MORE THAN YOU BARGAINED FOR.

"YOU'RE USED TO DEALING WITH HEROES...BUT WHAT YOU DON'T HAVE MUCH EXPERIENCE WITH IS *KINGS.*

"AND THAT'S YOUR PROBLEM HERE.

"YOU CAN'T THINK OF THEM AS NORMAL MEN. YOU CAN'T EVEN THINK OF THEM AS BEHAVING HUMAN--THAT'S THINKING TOO SMALL...

"THEY ARE LARGER THAN THAT, *BIGGER* THAN THAT...THEY EXIST ABOVE OTHER MEN BECAUSE THEY WERE BORN THAT WAY.

"AUTHORITY BEGAN AT THE CRADLE, YOU SEE.

"THEIR VERY IDEA OF MORALITY IS DIFFERENT THAN WHAT YOU ARE USED TO.

"THE PEOPLE--THEIR PEOPLE--EXPECT THEM TO DO VIOLENCE TO ENSURE A CERTAIN AMOUNT OF PEACE AND PROSPERITY.

"AND LIKE GODS, THEY ARE ALSO EXPECTED TO COMMIT MURDER...SO THE PEOPLE CAN SLEEP AT NIGHT KNOWING THEY ARE PROTECTED.

"YOU'VE UNDERESTIMATED YOUR SITUATION, BLACK SWAN.

"YOU'VE UNDERESTIMATED WHAT YOU'RE DEALING WITH."

BUT THERE IS *SOME* GOOD NEWS.

AND WHAT IS THAT?

I COULD BE A KING.

"WAS IT DAMAGED BY WHATEVER THAT WAS THAT STRANGE CONJURED?"

NO. EVERYTHING LOOKS INTACT, INCLUDING THE SHIELDING MECHANISM.

DIAGNOSTICS ARE GREEN ACROSS THE BOARD...

THE BOMB IS BOTH STABLE AND FULLY OPERATIONAL.

ALL RIGHT THEN. THIS IS IT.

BE-BOOP!

IT DOESN'T HAVE...HAVE TO BE.

YOU... YOU DON'T HAVE TO DO THIS...

I WILL DO IT.

T'CHALLA, I...I DON'T KNOW WHAT TO--

WE'RE OUT OF TIME. AND THIS IS ALL THAT'S LEFT...

THERE IS NOTHING LEFT TO SAY.

THEN WHY HESITATE...IS THIS YET MORE OF YOUR MERCY, T'CHALLA?

WHEN I WAS YOUNGER, YOU TOLD ME TO ALWAYS CONSIDER MY ACTIONS, FATHER.

THIS... DEMANDS CONSIDERATION.

DOES IT?

THIS ACTION IS NOT ABOUT YOU, OR ME, OR EVEN OUR PEOPLE--WHO ALL BLACK PANTHERS HAVE SWORN TO PROTECT...

IT IS THE ENTIRE LINE. ALL THAT WE WILL BE!

I CAN'T.

I WANT TO DO THE RIGHT THING... FOR YOU, FATHER...FOR MY PEOPLE. BUT I CAN'T DO THIS.

WE WERE CURSED WHEN WE MADE THIS MACHINE...

WE WERE DAMNED THE VERY DAY WE THOUGHT IT WAS FOR MEN TO DECIDE THINGS SUCH AS THIS.

DAMNED, T'CHALLA?

PERHAPS THAT WOULD BE FITTING...

BUT YOU STILL HAVE TIME.

IT...IS WRONG...

AND I CANNOT DO IT, FATHER!

I CANNOT.

NO. YOU CHOOSE NOT TO-- IT IS YOUR CHOICE.

SO HERE IS MINE: THERE IS AN ETERNITY... AND IN IT, YOU ARE DEAD TO ME, AND TO US ALL.

YOU HAVE NO PEOPLE.

YOU ARE NO BLACK PANTHER.

YOU ARE NO LONGER MY SON.

I'M SORRY...I'M SORRY...

IT'S OKAY, T'CHALLA.

IT'S OKAY. I UNDERSTAND...

"WE ARE NOT BROTHERS"

EARTH-616.
INCURSION ZONE.

FALLEN AT BEST.

AND AT WORST...

MONSTERS, NAMOR? HAVEN'T WE SECRETLY *ALWAYS* BEEN? MEN LORDING OVER THE LIVES OF THEIR LESSERS? I WONDER NOW...

IF THE ROAD I HAVE TRAVELED ALWAYS LED ME HERE, WERE THE CHOICES ALONG THE WAY STILL ALL *MINE*?

I THINK THEY WERE.

I'M NOT A VICTIM. I'M NOT A PAWN. I CHOSE THIS.

FOR THEY HAVE ALWAYS BEEN *THE DARK ARTS*.

STRANGE ISN'T WRONG. WHAT WE DID WAS WITH OPEN EYES...

BUT WE MADE OUR CHOICE-- I MADE *MY CHOICE*...AND THEN *YOU* TOOK IT FROM ME.

I DIDN'T DO THIS. *YOU DID*.

BECAUSE YOU COULDN'T.

"OUR SUN. OUR GALAXY. AND, EVENTUALLY, THE UNIVERSE ITSELF.

"THIS IS SIMPLY HOW THINGS ARE.

NEW MEXICO.

JUST THIS AND WHATEVER'S ON PUMP THREE.

NEED TO SEE SOME I.D.

SURE. AND THANK YOU FOR THAT.

PFFSST!

THIS IS IT, BIG GUY... END OF THE WORLD.

THIS IS HOW I'M *FINALLY* GONNA GET YOU.

THREE HOURS UNTIL INCURSION.

THE SANCTUM SANCTORUM.

THANK YOU, WONG. THAT WILL BE ALL.

OF COURSE.

AND WONG...

YES, DOCTOR?

I HAVE SOMETHING THAT I... THAT...

YES?

AM I A GOOD MAN?

NO.

TWO HOURS UNTIL INCURSION.

THE JEAN GREY SCHOOL FOR HIGHER LEARNING.

"WHY DID YOU COME HERE, T'CHALLA?"

I ASKED MYSELF, IF I HAD ONE DAY LEFT...IF I HAD JUST ONE MOMENT REMAINING, WHERE WOULD I WANT TO BE?

I DID NOT THINK OF DUTY-- WHERE I SHOULD BE, OR EVEN MY HOME-- WAKANDA. I THOUGHT OF BEING HERE... AND WITH *YOU.*

WHO WOULD EVER BELIEVE I WAS A ROMANTIC?

THAT'S FUNNY. I ALWAYS THOUGHT YOU WERE THE MOST ROMANTIC MAN I HAD EVER KNOWN.

I OFTEN THINK ABOUT WHAT COULD HAVE BEEN...

AND HOW THE UNIVERSE FOUND SOMETHING SO BEAUTIFUL UNFIT FOR THE WORLD.

CASTLE DOOM.

IT'S LATE... ARE YOU SURE THIS IS THE RIGHT WAY TO DO THIS, REED?

WE AGREED ON A CERTAIN PROTOCOL, SUSAN.

SO I HONESTLY DON'T CARE **WHAT** TIME IT IS-- WE RADIOED AHEAD, GAVE THE PROPER CLEARANCE, AND AGAIN, AS AGREED, FOLLOWED ALL THE FORMS.

NOW I WANT TO CHECK ON **MY** DAUGHTER.

OUR BABY GIRL IS CURRENTLY LIVING WITH VICTOR VON DOOM, SO YOU DON'T HAVE TO CONVINCE ME THAT, IN THIS INSTANCE, GOOD PARENTING MEANS CONSTANT SUPERVISION AND COURSE CORRECTING...

BUT FIRST THERE WAS YOUR URGENCY TO CHECK ON FRANKLIN AND THE REST OF THE FOUNDATION KIDS, THEN, IN THE SAME DAY, TO FLY HALF-WAY AROUND THE WORLD TO SEE VAL.

AM I MISSING SOMETHING?

NO, SUSAN...

I'M JUST SEEING **ALL** OF MY FAMILY TODAY.

THE BLUE AREA
OF THE MOON.

ONE MINUTE
UNTIL INCURSION.

FIFTY SECONDS UNTIL INCURSION.

FORTY SECONDS...

THIRTY SECONDS...

TWENTY SECONDS...

TEN SECONDS...

VMMMM

INCURSION.

SO, YES...WE HAD BETTER FIND OUT WHAT HAPPENED, BECAUSE **NONE** OF US CAN LIVE WITH THIS IF WE DON'T.

T'CHALLA... MY FRIEND...I FEEL THE SAME WAY...

...BUT IF I'M HONEST, THEN I CAN'T HELP BUT CONSIDER--

BLACK BOLT? WHAT IS...

OH...OH, NO... OH MY GOD...

WHAT IS IT, REED? WHAT DID HE SAY?

HE...HE SAID: "WHERE'S..."

RISE, THE CABAL.

COVER GALLERY